Princess Margaret
1930 – 2002
= Antony,
Earl of Snowdon
b. 1930
(divorced 1978)

David,
Viscount Linley
b. 1961
= Serena
Stanhope
b. 1970

Charles
Armstrong-Jones
b. 1999

Margarita
Armstrong-Jones
b. 2002

Lady Sarah
Armstrong-Jones
b. 1964
= Daniel
Chatto
b. 1957

Samuel
Chatto
b. 1996

Arthur
Chatto
b. 1999

Andrew,
Duke of York
b. 1960
= Sarah
Ferguson
b. 1959
(divorced 1996)

Princess
Beatrice
of York
b. 1988

Princess
Eugenie
of York
b. 1990

Edward,
Earl of Wessex
b. 1964
= Sophie
Rhys-Jones
b. 1965

Lady Louise
Windsor
b. 2003

James,
Viscount Severn
b. 2007

A catalogue record for this book is available from the British Library

Published by Ladybird Books Ltd
80 Strand, London, WC2R 0RL
A Penguin Company

001



ISBN 978-0-72328-022-4
Printed in Italy

PICTURE CREDITS

The publisher would like to thank the following for their kind permission to reproduce their photographs:
Jacket (front l) 174291189 © AFP/Getty Images; Jacket (front r) © Pool/Photoshot; Jacket (back) © FilmMagic/Getty Images; title page © Rex Features; 6t © E.O. Hoppé/CORBIS; 6b © Hulton-Deutsch Collection/CORBIS; 7t © Daily Mail/Rex Features; 7b © Rex Features; 8t © CORBIS; 8c © Baron, Camera Press London; 8b © Reginald Davis/Rex Features; 9t © Getty Images; 9b © Rex Features; 10t © Bettmann/CORBIS; 10b © Getty Images; 11t © Pool Photograph/Corbis; 11b © Pool Photograph/Corbis; 12t © Hulton-Deutsch Collection/CORBIS; 12b © FilmMagic/Getty Images; 13 © FilmMagic/Getty Images; 14t © CORBIS; 14bl © John Stillwell/Pool/epa/Corbis; 14br © DYLAN MARTINEZ/Reuters/Corbis; 15 © AFP/Getty Images; 16t © Bettmann/CORBIS; 16b © Norman Parkinson/Sygma/Corbis; 17t © SIPA Press/Rex Features; 17b © CHAMUSSY/NIVIERE/SIPA/Rex Features; 18t © Norman Parkinson/Sygma/Corbis; 18b © Getty Images; 19t © Norman Parkinson/Sygma/Corbis; 19bl © Rpe/albert Nieboer/dpa/Corbis; 19br © Rex Features; 20t © Hulton-Deutsch Collection/CORBIS; 20b © Bettmann/CORBIS; 21t © Hulton-Deutsch Collection/CORBIS; 21b © Rex Features ; 22t © Rex Features; 22bl © Getty Images; 22br © AlamyCelebrity/Alamy; 23t © Rex Features; 23bl © Getty Images; 23br © Stephane Ruet/Sygma/Corbis; 24t © Associated Newspapers/Rex Features; 24b © Pool Photograph/Corbis; 25t © AFP/Getty Images; 25b © Getty Images; 26t © Middleton Family/Alamy; 26B © Allpix /Splash News/Corbis; 27t © Getty Images; 27bl © Getty Images; 27bc © Rex Features; 27bc © Getty Images; 27br © WireImage/Getty Images; 27b © Getty Images; 28t © Amer Ghazzal/Demotix/Corbis; 28b © Getty Images; 29t © AFP/Getty Images; 29b © AFP/Getty Images; 30 © TopFoto

A LADYBIRD SOUVENIR

# THE ROYAL FAMILY

# A Royal Heir

**Our current monarch, Queen Elizabeth II, has reigned for more than sixty years.** She is Head of State in the UK and Head of 15 other Commonwealth realms.

*Our Queen as a baby*

Yet when Elizabeth was born on 21 April 1926, she did not expect to become Queen. Elizabeth's grandfather, King George V, died in 1936 and the crown passed to her uncle, King Edward VIII. After reigning for less than a year, he gave up the throne in order to marry Wallis Simpson, an American divorcee.

King Edward's abdication meant that Elizabeth's father became King George VI in 1936. Elizabeth, just ten years old, was now first in line to the throne. One day, she would be Queen.

*The Royal Family on the day of King George VI's coronation, 1937*

*Princess Elizabeth visits Sagana Lodge, Kenya, 1952*

That day arrived on 6 February 1952, when Elizabeth was twenty-five years old. The Princess and her husband were in Kenya when she learned of her father's death. Elizabeth returned home as Queen.

During her reign, the Queen has had support from her family, including her husband, sister and mother. Sadly, the Queen's sister, Margaret, and mother, Elizabeth, died within weeks of each other in 2002. This was the same year as the Queen's Golden Jubilee, which celebrated her fifty years on the throne.

*The Queen Mother was adored by her family and lived to be 101 years old*

# THE QUEEN AND THE DUKE OF EDINBURGH

*Elizabeth's coronation*

**The coronation of Queen Elizabeth II took place at Westminster Abbey on 2 June 1953.** The daunting prospect of the life of public duty that lay ahead must have been eased by the presence of her husband by her side.

Princess Elizabeth had married Prince Philip of Greece and Denmark in 1947. Shortly before the wedding, he was given the title The Duke of Edinburgh.

*ung Royal Family at*
*ore House, Windsor, 1968*

By the time of the Queen's coronation, the couple had two young children. Prince Charles was born in 1948 and Princess Anne in 1950. Two more sons followed: Prince Andrew in 1960 and Prince Edward in 1964.

Royal life has always been busy for the Queen. Every day, there are documents to sign and ceremonies to attend. She also strives to foster friendship and negotiation between the diverse nations of her Commonwealth. For a young mother, juggling family life with such a busy work schedule must have been tough. But the Queen has remained equally devoted to her family and her duty over the course of her reign.

*Queen Elizabeth II reads the contents of her official boxes, 1959*

In 2012, the Queen marked sixty years on the throne with events throughout the year celebrating her Diamond Jubilee. Although now in her eighties, she still attends many engagements each year. Recently however, younger members of the Royal Family have taken on more royal duties to support Her Majesty.

*Some of the Royal Family at the Trooping of the Colour, 2013*

# THE PRINCE OF WALES

*Prince Charles was given the title of Prince of Wales when he was nine years old*

**The Queen's eldest son, Prince Charles, is Heir Apparent to the throne.** This means he will one day succeed the Queen and be King.

Born on 14 November 1948, Charles was the first royal to go to school rather than be educated at home.

On 29 July 1981, the Prince of Wales married Lady Diana Spencer at St Paul's Cathedral. The couple's children are Prince William, born in 1982, and Prince Henry (usually known as Harry), born in 1984. The young princes became second and third in line to the throne. Sadly, Charles and Diana divorced in 1996.

The Prince of Wales is the patron of many charities and in 1976 also founded The Prince's Trust, which helps disadvantaged children.

*The Prince and Princess of Wales on their wedding day, July 1981*

*Diana, Princess of Wales*

**The Princess of Wales**

Lady Diana Spencer was born on 1 July 1961. She married Prince Charles when she was just twenty. During her marriage, and after, the Princess of Wales was a much-loved public figure. She undertook a wide range of royal duties and worked with many charities.

Diana's life was cut tragically short when she was killed in a car accident in Paris in 1997, leaving behind her two young sons.

In 2005, the Prince of Wales married Camilla Parker Bowles. The wedding was a largely private occasion. Even so, there were still 800 guests at the reception!

Prince Charles holds many titles, including Duke of Rothesay, Earl of Carrick and Duke of Cornwall. Upon her marriage, Camilla decided to use the title The Duchess of Cornwall.

*The Duke and Duchess of Cornwall on their wedding day, 2005*

*Prince William as a boy*

# THE DUKE OF CAMBRIDGE

**As the eldest son of the Prince and Princess of Wales, William has always known that he will one day be King.** The second in line to the throne was born on 21 June 1982 and was given the name Prince William Arthur Philip Louis of Wales. The young prince attended Eton College before studying Geography at St Andrews University, Scotland. There, Prince William met his future wife, Catherine Middleton.

After completing his degree, the Prince attended the Royal Military Academy Sandhurst, before training as an RAF Search and Rescue pilot.

On 29 April 2011, the world watched as Prince William married Catherine Middleton at Westminster Abbey. Upon their marriage, the couple were given the titles The Duke and Duchess of Cambridge.

*The happy couple wave to the cheering crowd*

*William and Catherine leave hospital following the announcement that they are expecting a baby, December 2012*

# PRINCE HARRY

*The young prince*

**The younger son of the Prince and Princess of Wales was born on 15 September 1984.** He was christened Henry Charles Albert David, but he has always been known as Harry. The Prince was educated at Eton College, before taking a gap year – part of which was spent working at an orphanage in Lesotho, Africa.

In 2005, Prince Harry entered the Royal Military Academy Sandhurst to begin his training as an Army officer. Upon completion, Prince Harry joined the Household Cavalry and has twice served on the front line in Afghanistan.

*A soldier's life suits Prince Harry*

*Prince Harry marches during a military parade, Sandhurst, 2006*

Captain Wales, as he is known, is the first member of the Royal Family to see active combat since his uncle, the Duke of York, fought in the Falklands War. He believes that if other soldiers are expected to put their lives on the line then so should he, regardless of his royal status.

Harry is patron of several charities and organizations that reflect issues close to his heart. He also supports charities that meant a lot to his mother, such as the brain injury charity Headway. In 2006, the Prince, along with Prince Seeiso of Lesotho, founded Sentebale – a charity that helps vulnerable children in Lesotho, Africa.

*Prince Harry greets pupils of a school for blind children in Lesotho, 2013*

# The Princess Royal

*Princess Anne as a child*

**The Princess Royal is the only daughter of the Queen and the Duke of Edinburgh.** She was born on 15 August 1950. Formerly known as Princess Anne, she was given her present title of Princess Royal in 1987.

Initially educated at home at Buckingham Palace, Princess Anne then attended Benenden School in Kent from the age of thirteen.

Princess Anne undertook her first solo engagement when she was eighteen and today is associated with over 200 charities and organizations. She has a wide range of public roles and a very busy schedule.

**Captain Mark Phillips**
Princess Anne married Lieutenant (later Captain) Mark Phillips in 1973. The couple had two children, Peter and Zara, before divorcing in 1992. Later the same year, the Princess Royal married Commander Timothy Laurence (now Vice Admiral Laurence) of the Royal Navy.

*Princess Anne and Lieutenant Mark Phillips on their wedding day, 1973*

The Princess Royal is a keen horsewoman. At the 1976 Montreal Olympic Games, she was part of the British Olympic three-day eventing team.

*Princess Anne competing at the 1976 Olympics*

In 2012, as President of the British Olympic Association, she played a vital role in bringing the Olympics to London. Sebastian Coe, Chairman of the London Organising Committee, praised her passion and enthusiasm, saying, "When we have a board meeting at midday she has often opened two hospitals and a school by then. Her effort has been extraordinary."

The Princess Royal's daughter, Zara, has followed in her mother's sporting footsteps. In 2012, she also competed at the Olympic Games.

*The Princess Royal and the Duke of Edinburgh watch Zara compete at the London Olympic Games, 2012*

# PETER PHILLIPS

*Peter as a young boy*

**Peter Mark Andrew Phillips, son of the Princess Royal and Captain Mark Phillips, is the Queen's eldest grandchild.** Born on 15 November 1977, he, along with his sister, holds no royal title. This was said to be at the request of his parents, who were keen for their children to lead as normal a life as possible.

Peter prefers to keep a low public profile and does not carry out any royal duties. In May 2008, he married Canadian-born Autumn Kelly at St George's Chapel, Windsor. They have two daughters – the Queen's first great-grandchildren. Savannah Anne Kathleen was born on 29 December 2010 and Isla Elizabeth on 29 March 2012.

*A family outing to the Badminton Horse Trials, May 2013*

# ZARA TINDALL

**Peter's younger sister, Zara, was born on 15 May 1981.** Like her mother, Zara is a respected equestrian. At school, she excelled at sport, notably hockey, athletics and gymnastics.

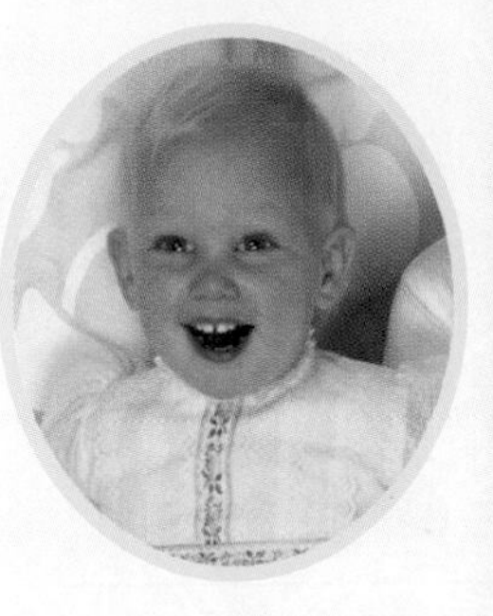

*Zara as a baby*

On 30 July 2011, Zara married her long-term partner, English rugby player Mike Tindall, at a ceremony in Edinburgh, Scotland. The couple are expecting their first child in 2014.

*Zara and Mike on their wedding day*

Zara competed in the London 2012 Olympic Games as part of the British Equestrian Team. The team came second in the eventing, making Zara the first British royal to win an Olympic medal.

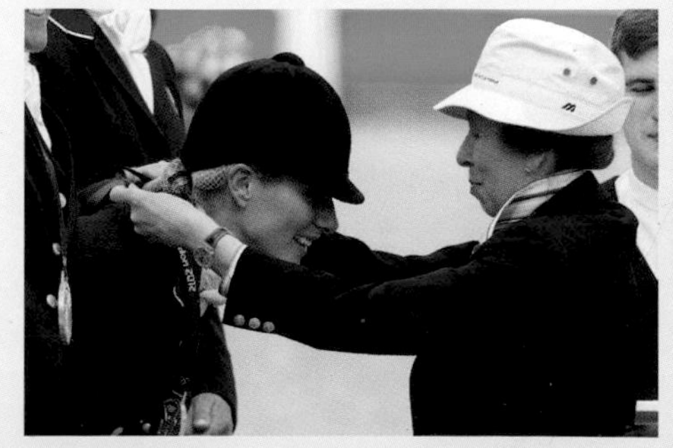

*Zara is presented with her silver Olympic medal by her mother*

# THE DUKE OF YORK

*Prince Andrew with his grandmother*

**Prince Andrew Albert Christian Edward, the Duke of York, is the Queen's third child.** Born on 19 February 1960, he joined the Royal Navy after leaving school in 1979. At the end of his training, not only had he earned his 'Wings' – meaning he was now qualified to fly – but was presented with the award for best pilot, too.

It was not long before Prince Andrew saw active service as part of the Task Force sent to regain the Falkland Islands in 1982. Throughout the conflict, the Prince flew on various missions, including Search and Air Rescue and casualty evacuation.

*Prince Andrew graduates from the Royal Naval College, Darmouth, 1980*

**The Duchess of York**

Sarah and Andrew wave to the crowd

Prince Andrew married Sarah Ferguson at Westminster Abbey on 23 July 1986. At the time of the marriage, he was given the title of The Duke of York and his wife The Duchess of York. The couple had two children, Beatrice and Eugenie, but divorced in 1996.

*The Duke of York abseils down The Shard, London, to raise money for charity, 2012*

After 22 years in the Royal Navy, Prince Andrew left active service to become a working royal. The Duke of York continues to support and maintain links with the military, as well as other charities and organizations, including arts patronages and tourist associations that promote Britain overseas.

# PRINCESS BEATRICE

*Princess Beatrice as a baby*

**Princess Beatrice Elizabeth Mary of York was born in London on 8 August 1988.** The young Princess attended St George's School in Ascot, and was made Head Girl in her final year. She went on to gain a degree in History and History of Ideas from Goldsmiths, University of London. Beatrice currently works for a venture capital firm in London.

The Princess is also involved with various charitable organizations, and in 2010 she became the first member of the Royal Family to complete the London Marathon. Beatrice and her friends dressed in green tutus and ran as Team Caterpillar!

*A fashionable princess*

*Team Caterpillar raised over £2 million for various charities*

# PRINCESS EUGENIE

**Princess Beatrice was followed on 23 March 1990 by her sister, Eugenie Victoria Helena.** She was the first royal baby to have a public christening, which was held at the local parish church of St Mary Magdalene at Sandringham Estate.

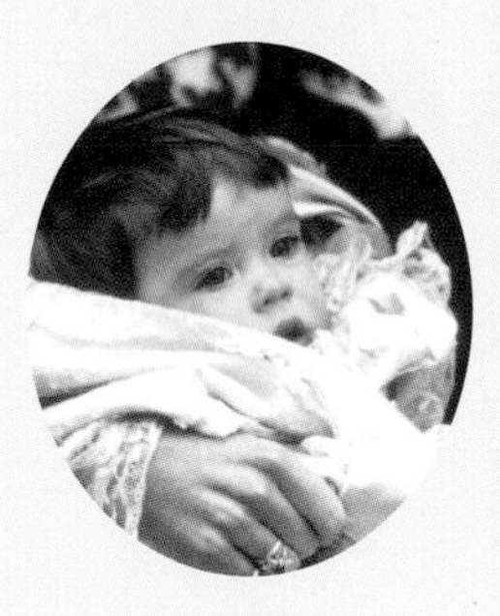

*The young Princess Eugenie*

After attending Marlborough College, Eugenie spent her university years in Newcastle studying English Literature, History of Art and Politics, graduating in 2012. In January 2013, Eugenie and her sister went to Germany on their first solo visit overseas, as part of the government campaign to promote Britain abroad.

*ugenie on her graduation day*

*Andrew, Sarah and their two daughters on holiday, 1998*

# The Earl and Countess of Wessex

*Prince Edward as a little boy*

**The Queen's youngest child, Prince Edward Antony Richard Louis, was born on 10 March 1964.** His introduction to royal life came early. His first public appearance was on the Buckingham Palace balcony after the Trooping of the Colour ceremony when he was just a few months old.

After finishing his school education, Prince Edward studied History at Cambridge University, while spending three years as a University Cadet in the Royal Marines. Prince Edward then worked at theatre and television production companies.

*The Earl of Wessex at a remembrance service, 2005*

In 2002, Edward announced that he would withdraw from his television production company to focus on supporting the Queen during the Golden Jubilee and beyond.

*The Earl and Countess of Wessex on their wedding day, 1999*

Prince Edward married Sophie Rhys-Jones in June 1999 and was given the titles of The Earl of Wessex and Viscount Severn. His wife became The Countess of Wessex. The royal couple have a daughter, Lady Louise, who was born in 2003, and a son, James, Viscount Severn, who was born in 2007.

*The happy family*

# THE DUCHESS OF CAMBRIDGE

*Catherine as a young girl*

**Catherine Elizabeth Middleton was born on 9 January 1982 and is the eldest of three children.** Educated at Marlborough College, she chose to head to the University of St Andrews in Scotland for her degree course. Little could she have realized the significance of this choice and how it would change the course of her life.

Before marrying Prince William, Catherine worked at her parents' party planning business. She also spent some time as a buyer for a clothing company. Since her marriage, Catherine's work within the Royal Family has involved supporting her husband and the Queen, as well as taking on several patronages of her own.

*Catherine meets a young boy while visiting the Art Room facilities at a primary school in Oxford, 2012*

In 2012, the Duchess played her part in the Queen's Diamond Jubilee and, along with her husband, was an Official Ambassador for Team GB and Paralympic GB during the Olympic and Paralympic Games in London.

*The Duchess was as excited as anyone to be a part of the Olympic celebrations*

On 3 December 2012, St James's Palace announced that the Duke and Duchess of Cambridge were expecting a baby. The pregnancy had a difficult start, as the Duchess was briefly admitted to hospital with acute morning sickness. Despite this, it was an exciting time for the royal couple and indeed the world, as everyone waited for the arrival of a new heir to the throne.

*The Duchess continues to attend public engagements during her pregnancy, 2013*

# THE PRINCE OF CAMBRIDGE

*The official announcement of the royal birth stands in the forecourt of Buckingham Palace, 2013*

**On 22 July 2013 at 4.24pm, the Duchess of Cambridge gave birth to a son.** Born at the Lindo Wing of St Mary's Hospital in London, the new baby weighed 8lb 6oz (3.74 kg). The third in line to the throne was given the name George Alexander Louis.

As word of the birth spread, the fountains in Trafalgar Square lit up blue and Times Square in New York displayed the news in lights. At one point over 25,000 tweets per minute were about the royal baby!

*Cannon shots fire in Green Park the day after the Prince's birth*

At 2pm the following day, the King's Troop Royal Horse Artillery staged a 41-gun salute in Green Park, London and the Honourable Artillery Company fired a 62-gun salute at the Tower of London. At the same time, the church bells of Westminster Abbey rang out for three hours.

*The world catches its first glimpse of the new baby, July 2013*

To celebrate the royal arrival, all babies born on the same day as Prince George of Cambridge were eligible to receive a silver penny made by the Royal Mint.

Over the last few years, fascination with the new, more modern, Royal Family has grown and the arrival of the royal baby was headline news around the world. William and Catherine will no doubt be eager to give their son as a normal childhood as possible, but as the years pass, His Royal Highness Prince George of Cambridge will take his first steps on the road to becoming King.